Leon Martin

Investing in Your Family

Leon Martin

Investing in Your Family
by Leon Martin

Cover design by Senir Design. Contact info:
info@senirdesign.com.

CLF Publishing Collaborative, LLC
Hesperia, CA 92345
Visit us at clfpublishing.org

First Edition: May 2026
ISBN 979-8-9925784-4-7 (paperback)

Dedications

To my father, Pastor Elihu Martin,
and my mother, Evangelist Ormie Martin,
of The Lord's House Church
and Triumph Temple Fellowship Church

Your lives have been a constant source of inspiration, guidance, and strength throughout my entire journey. Through your unwavering faith, steadfast commitment to God, and tireless service in ministry, you have modeled what it truly means to live a life devoted to purpose.
The foundation you laid, both spiritually and personally, has shaped who I am today. Your example of perseverance, integrity, and love for God's people has not only influenced my path, but has also become a guiding light in every season of my life.
This work is a reflection of the values you instilled, the prayers you prayed, and the legacy you continue to carry.

I honor you both with deep gratitude and love.

Acknowledgements

To my beloved late wife, Dr. Jacqueline Martin whose life, love, and unwavering faith remain woven into every page of this work. As co-founder of *Love, Peace, and Happiness Family Christian Fellowship* in 1974, she stood beside me with vision, strength, and a deep commitment to God's people. Together, we built not only a ministry, but a legacy grounded in love, service, and spiritual purpose. Her wisdom, grace, and steadfast devotion continue to inspire me, even in her absence. This book is, in many ways, a reflection of the seeds we planted together.

To our three children: Carlos, Devone, and Camille, I am profoundly grateful. Watching each of you walk in your own calling and serve in ministry in various capacities is a testimony to God's faithfulness and the foundation that was established in our home. Your commitment, your growth, and your dedication to advancing the Kingdom bring me immeasurable joy. You are living evidence that what is built in faith and nurtured with love will endure across generations. May this work honor the legacy we share and continue to impact lives for years to come.

To my lovely wife, Dr. Sheryl Martin for her constant love, encouragement, and support.

Contents

Foreword

by Dr. C.

It is both an honor and a joy to introduce *Investing in Your Family* by Bishop Leon Martin, a work that speaks to one of the most urgent and sacred needs of our time. In a world that often pulls families in opposing directions, this book calls us back to center, reminding us that the family is not merely a social unit, but a divine institution designed by God to nurture, strengthen, and sustain generations.

Bishop Martin writes not only with wisdom, but with lived experience. His voice carries the weight of years spent building, leading, and pouring into both his natural family and the broader family of faith. What makes this book especially powerful is its balance of spiritual insight and practical application. It does not remain in theory; it meets you where you are and equips you with tools to grow, heal, and build intentionally.

The concept of "investment" is both timely and necessary. Too often, families hope for strong relationships without making consistent deposits of time, communication, forgiveness, and love. Bishop Martin challenges that mindset, urging us to recognize that what we sow into our families today will determine the strength and stability of tomorrow. This book provides clear, actionable guidance for making those daily deposits that yield lasting fruit.

Throughout these pages, you will discover principles that address the core elements of family life: communication, spiritual alignment, relational health, and generational legacy. Each chapter serves as both a mirror and a roadmap: a mirror that reveals areas in need of attention and a roadmap that guides you toward meaningful transformation.

What I appreciate most is the heart behind this message. There is a genuine desire not just to inform, but to restore and strengthen families at every level. Whether you are leading a household, supporting one, or seeking to rebuild what has been strained, this book offers wisdom that is both accessible and deeply rooted in faith.

As you read, I encourage you to approach this book with openness and intention. Allow its principles to challenge you, its insights to guide you, and its truths to inspire action. Strong families do not happen by chance. Rather, they are built through consistent, purposeful investment.

I wholeheartedly recommend *Investing in Your Family* to you. May it serve as a catalyst for growth, a tool for restoration, and a source of enduring strength for your family and for generations to come.

Peace & Blessings,

Dr. C.

Introduction

The family is one of God's most sacred designs, a living, breathing expression of love, identity, and spiritual formation. It is within the family that values are first learned, character is shaped, faith is nurtured, and relationships are tested and refined. When functioning according to God's intent, the family becomes a place of safety, growth, and spiritual strength. When neglected, however, it can become a place of misunderstanding, distance, and emotional strain.

This book was written with one clear purpose: to provide practical and spiritual tools for building stronger family relationships and healthier communication. It is not merely a collection of ideas, but a guide rooted in biblical truth and applied wisdom, designed to help families move from surface-level interaction into meaningful connection, and from relational strain into intentional restoration.

At the heart of every strong family is communication. Yet communication is more than speaking and hearing; it is understanding, listening with discernment, responding with grace, and creating space for truth without fear. Many families do not struggle because of lack of love, but because of lack of tools, tools that help bridge emotional gaps, resolve conflict, and cultivate unity in everyday life.

The Scriptures remind us of the importance of building on a firm foundation. Matthew 7:24 teaches that the wise builder is the one who hears and acts upon God's Word, establishing a life that can withstand the pressures of storms. In the same way, families that are built on biblical principles are better equipped to endure seasons of challenge and change.

Within these pages, you will discover practical guidance for strengthening communication, fostering emotional and spiritual understanding, resolving conflict with wisdom, and cultivating a home environment where love is expressed consistently and intentionally. Each principle is designed to be lived, not merely read, applied in conversations, practiced in daily routines, and reflected in how family members treat one another.

This journey is not about achieving perfection within the home, but about pursuing transformation within it. Every family has room to grow, heal, and deepen its connection. Whether your family is experiencing harmony or tension, closeness or distance, this book offers tools to help you build, rebuild, and strengthen what matters most.

Ultimately, the goal is to see families become places where God's presence is welcomed, His wisdom is followed, and His love is reflected in every interaction. As you engage with these teachings, may your home be strengthened, your relationships restored, and your communication transformed, so that your family becomes what God intended it to be: a strong spiritual foundation for generations to come.

Chapter One

Investment Tips for Growing Your Family Relationships

Chapter One
Investment Tips for Growing Your Family Relationships

Warren Buffett is one of the richest men in America, and not just by accident or luck, but by discipline, patience, and wisdom in investing. In 1997, among the 70 or so people in this country who were worth 1 billion dollars or more, Buffett was the only one of only a few who acquired his wealth through investing, by carefully choosing where to place his resources, thinking long-term rather than short-term. Many investors look to him for investment advice because his track record speaks with unusual clarity and consistency. His firm, Berkshire Hathaway, has one of the most widely read annual reports issued, not merely because of financial data, but because of the wisdom and philosophy behind it. And a book has been written about his investment strategies; it's called *The Warren Buffett Way*, a guide that distills his principles into lessons others can follow.

If you could sit down with Warren Buffett for a while and get some investment tips, would you? Most people wouldn't hesitate. We instinctively recognize the value of learning from someone who has mastered the art of growing wealth.

Imagine for a moment that your family is your greatest capital. Not your job, not your portfolio, not your possessions, but your relationships. If you could get some investment tips on how to grow it in quality, depth, and strength, would you be interested? The return on that kind of investment is not measured in dollars, but in trust, joy, stability, and love, things far more enduring than financial gain.

We hold in our hands a treasure of investment strategies for growing our family relationships. The Bible, God's Word in written form, contains countless pro-family principles and precepts. These timeless truths that have guided generations through both prosperity and hardship. If we learn and practice them, not merely hearing but applying them, they will make our families relationally wealthy in ways that cannot be lost or taken away.

This chapter will cover just a few of the tips, which are simple in wording, but profound in impact.

Tip One: Understand Each Other

Did you once own a VCR? Did you know how to program it? There is a big difference between owning something and understanding how it works. Many people once had the device sitting in their living room, blinking "12:00," never quite unlocking its full potential. People who have a nodding acquaintance with a second language know the gap between hearing words and understanding the meaning of those words. You can hear sounds without grasping significance; you can be present without being connected.

1 Peter 3:7 (NASB) states, *"You husbands likewise, live with your wives in an understanding way, as with a weaker vessel, since she is a woman; and grant her honor as a fellow heir of the grace of life, so that your prayers may not be hindered."* This is not a casual suggestion; it is a direct instruction that carries spiritual weight.

Husbands, we are directly instructed to understand our wives. Now, I know some husbands who would say that it would be easier to understand quantum physics than to understand their wives. And guys, I know some wives who would say the same thing about us! That humorous tension points to a deeper truth: people are complex, and understanding takes effort.

Now while the text is directly addressed to husbands, it is not bad biblical interpretation to suggest that the principle of understanding one another can be applied to other relationships as well, such as parents and children, siblings, friends. Every meaningful relationship thrives on understanding.

What does it mean to understand another person? It means to "make what is important to the other person as important to you as the other person is to you." It is stepping into their world, seeing through their eyes, and valuing what they value, even when it doesn't come naturally to you.

For instance, one father who was not much of a sports fan had a son who developed an interest in hockey. So, one year, he took his son to as many hockey games as he could. It cost him some money and time, and likely a bit of personal discomfort, but it proved to be a strong bonding experience for them. One of his friends asked him in the midst of the hockey season, "Do you like hockey that much?" He said, "No, but I like my son that much!" That statement captures the heart of understanding, and it prioritizes the person over the preference.

How do we develop an understanding spirit? By making the time to really get to know each other - not superficially, but intentionally. And by making it a point to really listen to each other, not just waiting for our turn to speak, but seeking to comprehend. I believe it was Yogi Berra who said, "You can hear an awful lot by just listening." That kind of listening requires patience, humility, and focus.

James 1:19 (NLT) states that we should be *"quick to listen, slow to speak and slow to become angry."* That order is important. Listening comes first. Parents, I don't know of any child that would be repulsed by a parent who was quick to really listen to them. In fact, many children are quietly longing for exactly that. They desire to be heard, to be understood, and to be known.

Understanding is not automatic. It is an investment. But when it is made consistently, it yields deep connection and lasting trust.

Tip Two: Keep Commitments

It has been said we should be "generous with praise, but cautious with promises." That wisdom reminds us that words are easy to give, but promises carry weight. Parents, we need to do everything we can to keep promises we make to our children. Spouses, we need to do everything we can to keep our promises to one another. Children, you need to do everything you can to keep your promises to your parents. Every commitment, no matter how small it may seem, contributes to the overall strength of a relationship.

Why is keeping our commitments and honoring our promises so important? Because we all tend to construct our hopes around promises. Promises give shape to our expectations and stability to our emotions.

When a man promises to love a woman until death they do part, that gives the woman security to become all she was meant to be in the marriage relationship. It creates an environment where vulnerability feels safe and growth feels possible.

Ecclesiastes 5:4-5 (NLT) says, *"So when you make a promise to God, don't delay in following through, for God takes no pleasure in fools. Keep all the promises you make to him. It is better to say nothing than to promise something that you don't follow through on."* The seriousness of that warning reminds us that promises are not to be taken lightly.

We can infer from this text that the same holds true in our commitments to others. In other words, we are to be loyal. Proverbs 3:3-4 (NLT) says, *"Never let loyalty and kindness get away from you! Wear them like a necklace; write them down within your heart. Then you will find favor with both God and people, and you will gain a good reputation."* Loyalty, when consistently practiced, becomes part of our character.

When we keep our commitments, it builds trust. And there is no such thing as a healthy relationship apart from trust. Trust is the firm foundation upon which a family is built; it is what allows people to relax, to open up, and to rely on one another.

But keeping commitments can be costly. I remember one time this past year I was invited to a dinner meeting where the pastor of the largest Protestant church in America was going to be speaking. I really wanted to go, but when I looked at my calendar, I saw that I had made a previous commitment to some students in our church. That was tough for me, but I felt my previous commitment was more important. In that moment, I had to decide what kind of person I wanted to be, one who chases opportunities, or one who honors commitments.

I know some parents in the church who travel as a part of their profession. They will drive all night long in order to make it to a child's school program they promised they would be at. You can be assured when the child sees them, not only are they happy, but that parent has instilled within the child the importance of keeping commitments. That lesson will stay with them long after the event is over.

Do you have any commitments that need to be kept? Husbands and wives, when was the last time we revisited the vows (a.k.a., commitments) we made on our wedding day? When we married, we made a commitment that next to God, our spouse would be the most important relationship in our lives. Does our time and attention reflect that? If not, perhaps it is time to realign our priorities with our promises.

Tip Three: Give Respect

R.E.S.P.E.C.T. is not just something Aretha Franklin wanted; it is something all of us in any relationship want. It is a universal need, woven into the fabric of how we relate to one another. In fact, it is next to impossible to have a deep and lasting relationship with another person when there is no respect. Without it, communication breaks down, trust erodes, and emotional distance grows.

Could it be the reason some of us are not experiencing the kind of relationship God wants to have with us is because we do not have respect for Him? And could it be that the reason some family relationships are not secure is because God is not respected? Proverbs 14:26 (NLT) states, *"Those who fear (or respect) the Lord are secure; he will be a place of refuge for their children."* Respect for God doesn't just affect an individual. Rather, it creates a ripple effect that strengthens entire families.

Another word for respect is "honor." Romans 12:10 states that as Christ followers we are to take delight in honoring each other. Did you catch that? We are to *delight* in honoring another person. That means it should not feel like a burden, an obligation, or something we reluctantly do when we have to. Instead, it should be something we pursue with joy, because we recognize the value of the other person. When we delight in honoring another person, it boosts their sense of worth and reinforces their place in the relationship.

How can we show that we are honoring the people in our family relationships?

- By respecting each other's property
- By respecting each other's privacy
- By respecting each other's time

These may seem like small things, but they communicate big messages. When you knock before entering a room, you are saying, "You matter." When you return something you borrowed in good condition, you are saying, "I value what belongs to you." When you show up on time, you are saying, "Your time is important to me."

The people who have the most difficulty respecting others are those people with an inflated idea of their own importance, the sinfully proud. Pride places self at the center and diminishes others. Philippians 2:3 tells us to be humble, thinking of others as better than ourselves. Don't think only about your own affairs, but be interested in others, too, and what they are doing. Humility opens the door for respect, and respect strengthens every relationship it touches.

Tip Four: Offer Encouragement

Perhaps the easiest way to grow a healthy relationship is to offer encouragement, yet what appears simple on the surface carries profound and lasting impact when practiced consistently and intentionally. A well-known actress once said, "We live by encouragement, and we die without it, slowly, sadly and angrily." That statement captures the emotional and spiritual reality of the human condition: People flourish where affirmation is present, and they wither where it is absent.

1 Thessalonians 5:11 (NIV) says, *"Therefore encourage one another and build each other up, just as in fact you are doing."* Notice the dual command: not only are we to encourage, but we are also to actively build up. Encouragement is not passive; it is a deliberate act of strengthening another person's heart, confidence, and sense of worth. It is both spoken and demonstrated, and it must be ongoing "just as in fact

you are doing" suggesting that encouragement should become a lifestyle, not a rare event.

How can we encourage one another in our homes? How can we create an atmosphere where every family member feels seen, valued, and uplifted rather than diminished or overlooked?

- *By smiling*

Job, a man acquainted with grief and sorrow, in Chapter 29 of the book that bears his name, was recalling the days before he was visited with calamity. He said when people around him were discouraged, *"I smiled at them. My look of approval was precious to them"* (NLT). Even in recalling his past influence, Job reveals something powerful: Encouragement does not always require words. Sometimes, it is communicated through presence, expression, and silent affirmation.

Never underestimate the power of a smile. A smile not only increases your face value, but it warms the heart of those you give it to. It can disarm tension, communicate acceptance, and silently say, "You matter." In a home, a simple smile can shift the emotional climate from cold to comforting, from distant to connected.

- *By our words*

Someone noted, *"Man doesn't live by bread alone. He also needs buttering up."* While the phrase may sound humorous, it reveals a deep truth: People hunger for life-giving words. Words are power in that they can do enormous harm and amazing good. They can wound deeply or heal profoundly. They can tear down identity or reinforce it.

In the home, our words should be chosen carefully and spoken graciously. Encouraging words affirm effort, recognize growth, and call out potential. They remind others of who they are and what they can become. A consistent flow of kind, uplifting speech creates an environment where people feel safe, motivated, and loved.

- *By pointing out the positive*

A reporter once asked Andrew Carnegie, the great entrepreneur of the previous generation, why he hired 43 millionaires to work for him. Carnegie pointed out that those men were not millionaires when he hired them.

The reporter then asked, "How did you develop these men to become so valuable to you that you paid them so much money?"

Carnegie replied that people are developed the same way gold is mined. When gold is mined, several tons of dirt must be moved to get an ounce of gold; but you don't go into the mine looking for dirt; you go in looking for gold! This is a powerful analogy for our relationships. Too often, we focus on the "dirt," the flaws, mistakes, and shortcomings of those around us instead of the invaluable, God-given potential buried within them.

Start today to look for gold in your child, in your spouse, and in your parents. Look for the character, talents, and beauty that often lie beneath the surface of daily stress and human imperfection. Jesus certainly must have seen the gold in the disciples he chose, not what they were, but what they would become.

By giving gifts and, more importantly, by giving of ourselves, we help cultivate that precious metal. Are there any Barnabas' in your house? We desperately need more people who bring out the best in others. In Acts 4:36-37 we read there was a man named Joseph, the one the apostles nicknamed Barnabas (which means "Son of Encouragement"). He was from the tribe of Levi and came from the island of Cyprus. He sold a field he owned and brought the money to the apostles for those in need. Joseph, because of his behavior, was given the nickname "Son of Encouragement." One of the ways he practiced encouragement [was] by giving gifts. He understood that true encouragement often requires tangible sacrifice to lift the burden off someone else.

Tip Five: Ask For and Offer Forgiveness

Anyone who lives in a family of any kind knows that people will disappoint and hurt you. Unmet expectations and inconsiderate actions are inevitable. I asked my mom and dad, who had been married for 60 years, what were the secrets to their long and happy marriage. One gem of wisdom was "you overlook [a] lot of little things and you forgive each other." This doesn't mean ignoring serious issues, but choosing not to build a monument to every minor offense.

Colossians 3:13 (NLT) states: Bear with each other and forgive whatever grievances you may have against one another. Forgive as the Lord forgave you. Forgiveness is not natural. It seems to be more natural to carry a grudge; to record all wrongs in [red] on a legal pad in our minds; to think of ways of getting back at those who hurt us. It takes supernatural grace to break the cycle of resentment. Yet the Bible is clear in its instruction. As we have experienced forgiveness from God we are to forgive others.

The Spanish have a story about a father and son who became estranged. The son left home, and the father later set out to find him. He searched for months with no success. Finally, in desperation, the father turned to the newspaper for help. His ad simply read, "Dear Paco, meet me in front of this newspaper office at noon on Saturday. All is forgiven. I love you. Your father." The name Paco is common, and the plea was universal. On Saturday, eight hundred young men named Paco showed up looking for forgiveness and love from their estranged fathers. Families today are filled with people who desperately long for reconciliation. They are waiting for someone to take the first step, to say, "All is forgiven."

Some of you need to experience that kind of forgiveness from God. You can. God has sent out a letter of forgiveness – his name is Jesus. If you will receive him, forgiveness will be yours.

Chapter Two

A Recipe for Successful Parenting

Chapter Two
A Recipe for Successful Parenting

I made a startling discovery soon after our first child was born: children do not come with an instruction manual. Faced with this sudden realization, we did what many new parents do: we called our moms. The conversations sounded something like this: "Mom, she's doing this... is she supposed to do that?"

Most parents can relate to the story of a young student of child behavior who frequently delivered a lecture titled *"Ten Commandments for Parents."* After he married and had his first child, the lecture became *"Ten Hints for Parents."* When the second child arrived, it changed to *"Some Suggestions for Parents."* By the time the third child was born, the lecturer, so the story goes, stopped lecturing altogether.

The truth is, we often have the strongest opinions about raising children before we actually have any. We confidently declare, "My children will never do that!" Those words have a way of coming back to haunt us.

Humorist Mark Twain once offered this tongue-in-cheek advice: "When they become teenagers, put them in a barrel and feed them through the knothole. When they turn sixteen, plug up the knothole!"

Two children were once overheard discussing their parents. One said, "I'm really worried. Dad works tirelessly, so I can have everything I need and go to college someday. Mom works hard taking care of me, cleaning, cooking, and driving me everywhere. They spend all their time working for me. But I'm worried." His friend asked, "What do you have to worry about?" The first replied, "I'm afraid they're going to try to escape someday."

James Dobson once said, "Childrearing is like baking a cake; you don't realize you have a disaster until it's too late." But success in both parenting and baking is best achieved by following a good recipe. So, I would like to offer you *A Recipe for Successful Parenting.*

Ingredient One: Recognize Your Child as a Gift from God

If we are going to survive the challenges of parenting, we must remember that our children are gifts from God. Psalm 127:3–5 (NKJV) reminds us: *"Behold, children are a heritage from the Lord, The fruit of the womb is a reward. Like arrows in the hand of a warrior, So are the children of one's youth. Happy is the man who has his quiver full of them…"* Even when they test our patience, or seem determined to do the opposite of what we ask, our children are still a gift. If you want to endure the struggles of parenthood, hold tightly to that truth.

Ingredient Two: Practice Unconditional Love

We are called to love our children the way God loves us, with patience, grace, and consistency. Never allow your child to believe that your love is dependent on their behavior. Correction may be necessary, consequences may follow actions, but love must remain constant. A child who feels secure in their parents' love is far more likely to grow into a confident and emotionally healthy adult.

Ingredient Three: Recognize and Work with Your Child's Natural Bent

Parenting requires intentional training. Proverbs 22:6 (NKJV) says: *"Train up a child in the way he should go, And when he is old he will not depart from it."* This verse is often misunderstood as a guarantee. It is not a promise of perfect outcomes, but rather a principle of wise parenting. A helpful paraphrase might be: "Shape your child's training according to their unique, God-given traits and tendencies; when they mature, they will retain what they have learned."

Every child has natural inclinations, strengths and weaknesses, that make them unique. Effective parenting recognizes these differences rather than ignoring them.

Interestingly, the Hebrew root for "train up" refers to the palate or roof of the mouth. It was used to describe a midwife placing a sweet substance on a newborn's gums to stimulate the desire to feed. In the same way, parents are called to create a "thirst" in their children, for what is good, true, and godly (Swindoll, 1977).

Deuteronomy 6:5–7 reinforces this idea: *"You shall love the Lord your God with all your heart... And these words... shall be in your heart. You shall teach them diligently to your children..."* Children develop appetites based on what they are consistently exposed. One of the greatest responsibilities of a parent is to cultivate a desire in their children for what truly matters.

Ingredient Four: Practice Consistent Discipline

Discipline is one of the most challenging and most important responsibilities of parenting. Proverbs 29:15 (NKJV) says: *"The rod and rebuke give wisdom, But a child left to himself brings shame to his mother."* And Proverbs 29:17 (NKJV) adds: *"Correct your son, and he will give you rest; Yes, he will give delight to your soul."* Discipline, when done properly, produces wisdom, peace, and maturity. When neglected, it often results in confusion and heartache.

Some years ago the city of Houston Texas waged an ad campaign to deter juvenile crime, the Houston Police Department came up with "Twelve Rules for Raising Juvenile Delinquent Children."

1. Begin with infancy to give the child everything he wants. As a result, he will grow up to believe the world owes him a living.

2. When he picks up bad words, laugh at him. This will make him think that it is cute.
3. Never give him any spiritual training. Wait until he is twenty-one and then let him "decide for himself.'
4. Avoid use of the word "wrong." It may develop a guilt complex. This will condition him to believe later, when he is arrested for stealing a car, that society is against him and he is being persecuted.
5. Pick up everything he leaves lying around. Do everything for him, so that he will be experienced in throwing all responsibility on others.
6. Let him read any printed matter he can get his hands on. Be careful, that the silverware and drinking glasses are sterilized, but let his mind feast on garbage.
7. Quarrel frequently in the presence of your children. So, they won't be shocked when the home is broken up later.
8. Give a child all the spending money he wants. Never let him earn his own.
9. Satisfy his every craving for food, drink and comfort. See that every sensual desire is gratified.
10. Take his part against neighbors, teachers and policemen. They are all prejudiced against your child.
11. When he gets into real trouble, apologize for yourself by saying, "I never could do anything with him."

12. Prepare for a life of grief. You will likely have it (Swindoll, 1977, pp. 63-67).

Ephesians 6:4 (NKJV) provides balance: *"And you, fathers, do not provoke your children to wrath, but bring them up in the training and admonition of the Lord."*

The first word translated, "training" (paideia) it is the word we get pedagogy from. It can refer to discipline but normally contains the broader meaning of education, the entire training particularly of the very young.

The second word, "admonition" (nouthesia) comes from the combination of two Greek words one meaning "mind" and the other "to place" and involves the idea of reasoning and gentle or friendly reproof. It is more appropriate to the child as he gets older when they can have a better understanding of the spiritual and moral issues of their own behavior.

We must recognize the necessity of discipline. Here are some practical reminders for discipline:

- Never discipline in anger.
- Choose your battles wisely.
- Allow children to express emotions appropriately.
- Discipline privately, not publicly.
- Speak calmly and carefully.

Proverbs 15:1 reminds us: *"A soft answer turns away wrath, But a harsh word stirs up anger."* Yelling rarely produces growth; it often creates resentment. Calm, consistent discipline builds respect and understanding.

Ingredient Five: Be Willing to Admit When You Are Wrong

No parent is perfect. Mistakes are inevitable. When you make a mistake, admit it. Your children already know you are not perfect. What they need to see is humility, honesty, and accountability. When parents model this, children learn to do the same.

If your children are adults, your role is not over. You can invest in younger families, mentor new parents, and influence your grandchildren in meaningful ways.

A Final Word

The idea that good parents always produce good children, and bad parents produce bad ones, is simply not true. Life is more complex than that. We have all seen examples of both:

- Dysfunctional homes where children grow into responsible adults
- Godly homes where children make poor choices

Scripture provides principles, not guarantees. However, parents who consistently apply these principles, recognizing their children as gifts, loving unconditionally, training wisely, disciplining consistently, and living humbly, are far more likely to raise children who grow into strong, responsible, and faithful adults.

The foundation is simple, though not easy:

- Know God's Word.
- Live it out daily.
- Pray consistently.
- Love deeply.
- Take nothing for granted.
- And hold firmly to your faith.

That is a recipe worth following.

Chapter Three

What God Can Do For Your Family

Chapter Three
What God Can Do For Your Family

Think of Dorothy in *The Wizard of Oz* who said, *"There's no place like home."* And she was right. There's no place like home... when it is happy and healthy. A happy, healthy home is one of the greatest places on earth. But an unhappy, unhealthy home can become one of the most painful environments a person will ever experience. The question is simple, but deeply important: *How can we build a happy and healthy home?*

Let's answer that question directly from the Bible. There are several steps we must take, and turning to God is the first step. Someone might ask, *"What can God really do for my family?"* That's a fair question, and Psalm 127 gives us a clear and powerful answer.

This psalm is traditionally attributed to Solomon, but many believe it reflects the wisdom passed down from his father, David. Either way, it offers timeless, godly insight into building a family. In this short psalm, we find four essential truths about what God can do for any family that turns to Him.

I. God Can Help Me BUILD My Family

"Unless the Lord builds the house, the builders labor in vain" (Psalm 127:1, NIV). The "house" here isn't just a structure; it represents a home, a family, a legacy. Without God, even our best efforts fall short. We may work hard, read books, attend seminars, and try every strategy available, but if God is not at the center, we are building on a shaky foundation.

God is the original designer of the family. He knows what works and what doesn't. Think about it this way: A story is told about Henry Ford. One day, he and his wife came across a man stranded with a broken-down Model T. Ford stopped, examined the car, and within minutes had it running again. The owner was amazed. "How did you fix it so quickly?" he asked. Ford replied, "Because I'm the one who designed it."

That's exactly how it is with God and the family. God says, "I designed it; I know how to fix it." Now, God doesn't magically transform marriages or children overnight. He doesn't wave His hand and turn families into perfect sitcom households, like Ward and June Cleaver. Nor will He wave His hand over your children and transform them into the Brady kids. Instead, He provides something better: the necessary instructions and tools and says, "Here's what you need. Get to work. I'll help you every step of the way."

Where do we find that guidance? In the Bible. Scripture is the most time-tested manual for marriage and parenting ever written. It has guided millions of families across generations. But, like any instruction manual, it only works if you actually follow it.

Think about the wise man who built his house on the rock that is mentioned in Matthew 7. A strong home isn't built on convenience or culture. It's built on obedience to God's Word. If you want God to build your family, commit to learning His truth and living it out daily. Follow His instructions, and He will help you BUILD your family.

II. God Can Help Me PROTECT My Family

"Unless the Lord watches over the city, the guards stand watch in vain" (Psalm 127:1, NIV). A city is made up of families, and the word "watches" means to guard, protect, and preserve.

There was an ADT commercial where a burgular is trying to break into a home and oldest daughter pushes the panic button and frightens the burgular away.

Not only does your family need protection from burglars and prowlers, it also needs protection from evil spiritual forces. You see, the devil and his demons would love nothing more than to break up and destroy your family. The enemy seeks to divide, weaken, and ultimately destroy families. And he often uses subtle, socially accepted tools to do it.

A. Alcohol

Alcohol is a cold-blooded killer and has destroyed countless homes. It has killed families. It has killed marriages. It damages judgment, weakens self-control, and often leads to broken relationships. Parents, if you have alcohol in your house, then you are housing a cold-blooded killer! In fact, you better off having Charles Manson as a house guest. At least he'd be quick about it - while the bottle takes it's time in killing your family.

Patterns tend to repeat across generations. Children often imitate what they see. When parents normalize harmful behaviors, children are more likely to adopt them. God's protection sometimes looks like giving you the strength to say *no* to break cycles that could otherwise continue for generations.

B. Adultery

There is only one sin that can break the marriage bond in the eyes of God: the sin of adultery. The devil and his demons will do everything they can to get you to be unfaithful to your spouse. But God can protect your family by helping you be faithful and committed to your mate. Faithfulness isn't just a feeling; it's a daily decision. God strengthens that commitment when you seek Him, honor Him, and guard your heart.

C. Selfishness

This is Satan's most successful weapon against the home. A "me-first" attitude quietly erodes a home from the inside. When each person focuses only on their own needs, love begins to disappear. God calls us to something better: a Christ-like attitude that values others above ourselves. A home marked by humility, sacrifice, and love is a home that stands strong. If you invite God into your family life and follow His ways, He will actively help protect what matters most.

III. God Can Help Me PROVIDE for My Family

Psalm 127:2 paints a picture of two different approaches to provision: *"In vain you rise early and stay up late, toiling for food to eat - for he grants sleep to those he loves."*

Do you know how God provides for your family? He doesn't send food down from heaven like He did for the Israelites so long ago. Instead, He provides through good old fashioned work. He tells us to provide for our families by earning a good honest living.

This verse describes two types of fathers who try to provide for their families. The first father can't sleep at night because he isn't content with what he has. He works long hours in order to provide his family with the luxuries of life. The second father can sleep at night, not because he's lazy, but because he's content with what he has. He works in order to provide his family with the necessities of life - and he's content with that.

Mothers and fathers, we need to learn the difference between luxuries and necessities. Children don't need lots of toys, designer clothes, and swimming pools. Those things are luxuries. Children need a roof over their head, food on their table, and clothes on their back. They need your attention, your affection, your guidance, and your good example. They need to be disciplined in love. They need to know that they are important to you, that you love them, and you enjoy spending time with them. Those are necessities.

If you can provide both the luxuries and necessities, more power to you. But most parents have to make a choice. Don't be like the first father mentioned in verse 2. Be like the second father and provide what your children NEED instead of what they WANT. And you will find contentment and peace of mind.

They need:

- Stability
- Love
- Attention
- Guidance
- Consistent discipline
- A godly example

Those are the true essentials of a healthy home. There's nothing wrong with enjoying blessings when you can, but not at the cost of your presence, your peace, or your priorities. A content home is often a healthier home than a wealthy but disconnected one.

IV. God Can Help Me RAISE My Family

"Children are a heritage from the Lord, offspring a reward from him" (Psalm 127:3, NIV).

Children are not a burden; they are a blessing. In a culture that sometimes treats children as obstacles to success or personal freedom, Scripture offers a radically different perspective: children are a gift entrusted to us by God. They don't make life poorer; instead, they make it richer in ways money never can. Verses 4–5 compare children to arrows in the hands of a warrior. An arrow must be shaped, guided, and aimed before it is released. In the same way, children must be taught, guided, and nurtured while they are young and impressionable.

The early years matter. Values are not primarily taught through lectures. They are learned through example. Children watch more than they listen. They absorb what they see in your actions, your priorities, your attitudes, and your faith.

If you want your children to grow up with strong values:

- Live what you believe
- Model integrity
- Demonstrate love and respect
- Make your faith visible and authentic

Teach them with your words, but confirm it with your life.

A Final Word

Parents, where are you today? If you don't have a personal relationship with Jesus, these principles can improve your home, but they cannot secure your eternity. A transformed family begins with a transformed heart. Salvation is not about religion; it's about a relationship.

If you're ready to begin that relationship, you can pray: "Dear Lord, I know I need you. I believe Jesus died for my sins and rose again. I give my life to you. Forgive me, change me, and help me live for you every day."

And if you already know Him, then make this your prayer: "Dear Lord, I love my family. Help me to put you first. Teach me to build, protect, provide for, and raise my family according to Your will."

Chapter Four

Investing in the Family: Part One

The Family is Your Greatest Asset

Chapter Four
Investing in the Family: Part One
The Family is Your Greatest Asset

In a world driven by money, success, and personal achievement, many people overlook the most valuable investment they will ever have: their family. Stocks rise and fall. Businesses come and go. But the family, when properly nurtured, produces generational wealth that cannot be measured in dollars. This kind of wealth shows up in character, faith, resilience, and legacy. These are things no market can crash and no economy can take away.

A strong family is not built accidentally; it is built intentionally. Daily choices, attitudes, and priorities shape the atmosphere of a home more than occasional grand gestures ever could.

Genesis 2:24 (KJV) says, "*Therefore shall a man leave his father and his mother, and shall cleave unto his wife...*" From the very beginning, God established the family as a covenant relationship, one marked by unity, loyalty, and intentional connection. This verse highlights that family is not passive; it requires commitment and action.

Just like any investment, the family requires time, attention, and consistent deposits. You cannot expect a return where there has been no contribution. Many people invest hours into careers but give leftovers to their loved ones. Over time, this imbalance weakens the very foundation that supports everything else in life. What seems urgent often replaces what is truly important.

A healthy family provides:

- Emotional stability
- Spiritual covering
- Identity and belonging
- Strength during adversity

These are not small benefits. They are essential to a flourishing life. Emotional stability gives peace, spiritual covering provides direction, identity shapes confidence, and strength during adversity sustains perseverance.

When the family is strong, individuals are strong. When the family is broken, society feels the impact. Mark 3:25 (KJV) says, *"And if a house be divided against itself, that house cannot stand."* This truth extends beyond the home; it affects communities, nations, and future generations. The question is not *if* you are investing in your family. The question is what kind of investment are you making?

Joshua 24:15 (KJV) says, *"As for me and my house, we will serve the Lord."* This declaration is a decision of leadership and intentionality. It sets the tone for the entire household, establishing spiritual direction and purpose.

Are you investing:

- Time or distraction?
- Presence or absence?
- Love or neglect?

Every interaction is a deposit or a withdrawal. Words spoken in frustration can withdraw from the relationship, while words spoken in love can build it. Small, consistent deposits over time create strong relational equity.

The most successful families understand that love must be expressed, not assumed. Words of encouragement, quality time, and genuine care are the currency of strong relationships. Love that is not communicated can be misunderstood or even missed entirely.

If you want a thriving family, you must treat it like your most valuable portfolio, because it is. And unlike financial portfolios, the return on this investment carries eternal significance.

Building a Strong Foundation

Every successful structure begins with a solid foundation. The same is true for the family. Without a strong base, pressure, conflict, and life's storms will cause cracks that eventually lead to collapse. A weak foundation may not be obvious at first, but it will always reveal itself under pressure.

Matthew 7:24–25 (KJV) says, *"...a wise man, which built his house upon a rock... And the rain descended, and the floods came... and it fell not: for it was founded upon a rock."* This passage reminds us that storms are inevitable but collapse is not. The difference is the foundation.

There are three foundational pillars every family must establish:

1. Spiritual Alignment

A family grounded in faith has direction and stability. Spiritual alignment creates unity and gives each member a shared purpose. Without it, individuals may move in different directions, creating confusion and division.

Proverbs 3:5–6 (KJV) states: *"Trust in the Lord with all thine heart... and he shall direct thy paths."* When a family trusts God collectively, decisions become clearer and burdens become lighter.

This includes:

- Praying together
- Studying the Word together
- Seeking guidance from God in decisions

When God is at the center, the family gains strength beyond human ability. His wisdom fills the gaps where human understanding falls short.

2. Communication

Communication is the lifeline of the family. Many families don't fail because of lack of love. They fail because of lack of understanding. Miscommunication can create distance even when love is present.

Ephesians 4:29 (KJV) informs us, *"Let no corrupt communication proceed out of your mouth, but that which is good to the use of edifying..."* Words have the power to build up or tear down. Healthy families choose words that strengthen.

Healthy communication requires:

- Listening without interrupting
- Speaking truth with love
- Creating safe spaces for expression

Silence can be more damaging than conflict. When people stop talking, they start disconnecting. Honest, respectful dialogue keeps relationships alive and growing.

3. Commitment

Strong families are not built on convenience; they are built on commitment. Commitment holds the family together when emotions fluctuate and circumstances become difficult.

Galatians 6:9 (KJV) states, *"And let us not be weary in well doing: for in due season we shall reap, if we faint not."* Consistency in doing what is right produces long-term results.

Commitment says:

- "I'm here even when it's hard."
- "We will work through challenges."
- "We don't give up on each other."

In today's culture, commitment is often replaced with comfort. But growth never happens in comfort zones. Families grow stronger when they endure, forgive, and move forward together.

Hebrews 10:25 (KJV) says, *"Not forsaking the assembling of ourselves together..."* This principle applies within the home as well, staying connected, present, and engaged with one another. A solid foundation doesn't mean a perfect family. It means a resilient one. Strength is not found in perfection, but in perseverance.

The Power of Consistent Investment

Investment is not a one-time action. It is a lifestyle. The strength of a family is determined not by occasional efforts, but by consistent habits. What you do daily matters more than what you do occasionally. Luke 16:10 (KJV) tells us, *"He that is faithful in that which is least is faithful also in much..."* Faithfulness in small moments builds a strong and lasting family over time. Small, daily investments create lasting impact.

Time Is the Greatest Currency

You can't replace lost time. Being physically present is important, but being emotionally present is essential. Distraction can rob moments that could have built connection.

Simple moments matter:

- Family meals

- Conversations
- Shared experiences

These moments build memories that last a lifetime. Often, it is the ordinary days that leave the deepest impressions.

Discipline and Structure

Every strong family has structure. Discipline provides order and teaches responsibility. Without it, confusion and inconsistency take over.

Ephesians 5:23 (KJV) informs us, *"For the husband is the head of the wife, even as Christ is the head of the church..."* This reflects order, responsibility, and loving leadership, not control, but guidance rooted in care.

This includes:

- Setting expectations
- Establishing routines
- Holding each other accountable

Without structure, chaos enters. With discipline, growth happens. Structure creates an environment where everyone understands their role and responsibility.

Love in Action

Love is more than words; it is demonstrated through actions. Genuine love shows up consistently, especially when it is inconvenient.

1 Corinthians 13:7 (KJV) states, *"Beareth all things, believeth all things, hopeth all things, endureth all*

things." This kind of love is enduring, patient, and sacrificial.

Love looks like:

- Forgiveness when mistakes are made
- Patience during difficult seasons
- Support in times of need

Consistent love builds trust. And trust is the glue that holds the family together. Without trust, relationships weaken; with it, they flourish.

Generational Impact

What you invest today will show up tomorrow, not just in your children, but in generations to come. The seeds you plant now will grow into future realities.

Proverbs 22:6 (KJV) instructs: *"Train up a child in the way he should go..."* Intentional guidance shapes lifelong direction. You are not just raising a family; you are shaping a legacy. Your influence extends far beyond what you can currently see.

The habits you build...

The values you teach...

The love you give... will echo long after you are gone.

Legacy is not built in a moment. It is built over a lifetime of consistent investment.

Please Remember

Investing in the family is the most rewarding decision you will ever make. It requires sacrifice, patience, and intentionality, but the return is priceless. The rewards are not always immediate, but they are always meaningful and lasting.

Psalm 127:1 (KJV) informs us, *"Except the Lord build the house, they labour in vain that build it..."* Without God as the foundation, even the best efforts fall short. With Him, even imperfect efforts are strengthened. A strong family doesn't just happen. It is built - one day, one choice, and one investment at a time.

Chapter Five

Investing in the Family: Part Two

Building a Strong Family of Faith

Chapter Five
Investing in the Family: Part Two
Building a Strong Family of Faith

Families of faith today are facing pressures from many directions - some new, some longstanding but intensified by modern life. Here are some of the most significant challenges, expanded with deeper reflection and Scripture for guidance:

1. Erosion of Spiritual Priorities

Busy schedules, work demands, and constant distractions (especially from phones and media) often push prayer, Bible study, and church involvement to the margins. What used to be central can slowly become optional. Over time, this drift is rarely intentional. It happens subtly, through small compromises and the normalization of spiritual neglect. When God is no longer the focal point of daily life, families may find themselves spiritually depleted without fully realizing how they got there.

Scripture reminds us of the importance of guarding what matters most: *"But seek first the kingdom of God and His righteousness, and all these things shall be added to you"* (Matthew 6:33, NKJV). Prioritizing God is not about adding another task to a crowded schedule. Rather, it is about reordering life so that everything else flows from Him.

2. Cultural and Moral Shifts

Society's values are rapidly changing, often conflicting with biblical principles. Issues around identity, truth, marriage, and morality can create confusion, especially for children and teens trying to reconcile faith with what they see in culture. Without clear guidance, young people may adopt beliefs shaped more by culture than by Scripture.

The Bible cautions against conforming to shifting cultural norms: *"And do not be conformed to this world, but be transformed by the renewing of your mind..."* (Romans 12:2, NKJV). Families are called not only to resist cultural drift but to actively cultivate a biblical worldview grounded in truth and love.

3. Digital Distractions & Influence

Social media and entertainment shape beliefs, attitudes, and behaviors. Families are competing with powerful digital voices that often contradict faith-based teaching, making it harder to disciple children at home. Constant exposure to curated lifestyles and opinions can distort reality, foster comparison, and weaken spiritual focus.

Scripture emphasizes the importance of guarding the heart and mind: *"Keep your heart with all diligence, for out of it spring the issues of life"* (Proverbs 4:23,

NKJV). Being intentional about media consumption and creating tech boundaries can help families protect what influences their thinking and values.

4. Breakdown of Family Structure

Single-parent households, divorce, and generational gaps can strain stability. When the family unit is under pressure, spiritual growth and consistency can suffer. Even in intact families, relational disconnection can weaken the sense of unity and shared purpose.

God's design for family emphasizes strength and mutual support: *"Therefore what God has joined together, let not man separate"* (Mark 10:9, NKJV). While brokenness exists, God's grace also restores, and families can find healing and strength through Him.

5. Lack of Consistent Discipleship at Home

Many families rely on church alone for spiritual growth, but without daily teaching and modeling at home, faith can become shallow or inconsistent. Children learn not only from what is taught but from what is lived out. When faith is not integrated into everyday life, it risks becoming compartmentalized.

Scripture places the responsibility of discipleship within the home: *"And these words which I command you today shall be in your heart. You shall teach them diligently to your children..."* (Deuteronomy 6:6–7, NKJV). Faith is strengthened when it is woven into daily conversations, decisions, and relationships.

6. Financial Pressure and Stress

Rising costs of living and economic uncertainty create anxiety. Financial stress can lead to conflict, distraction, and less focus on spiritual matters. Worry about provision can overshadow trust in God's faithfulness, creating tension within the household.

The Bible encourages reliance on God rather than fear: *"And my God shall supply all your need according to His riches in glory by Christ Jesus"* (Philippians 4:19, NKJV). Practicing stewardship, contentment, and trust can help families navigate financial challenges with peace.

7. Mental Health Challenges

Anxiety, depression, and emotional struggles are increasing, even among believers. Families may struggle with how to address these issues while holding onto faith and hope. Ignoring these struggles can lead to isolation, while addressing them with wisdom and compassion can foster healing.

Scripture speaks to God's nearness in times of distress: *"Casting all your care upon Him, for He cares for you"* (Peter 5:7, NKJV). Faith and practical support, such as counseling, community, and honest conversation, can work together in the healing process.

8. Busyness and Overcommitment

Sports, work, school, and activities leave little time for meaningful connection. Families may live under the same roof but lack real fellowship and spiritual bonding. Overcommitment often leads to exhaustion, making it difficult to invest in what truly matters.

The Bible reminds us to be intentional with our time: *"See then that you walk circumspectly, not as fools but as wise, redeeming the time..."* (Ephesians 5:15–16, NKJV). Slowing down and creating space for connection allows relationships and faith to grow deeper.

9. Decline in Church Engagement

Regular attendance and involvement are decreasing in many places, weakening community support, accountability, and spiritual covering. Without consistent fellowship, families may feel isolated in their faith journey and lack encouragement during difficult times.

Scripture highlights the importance of gathering together: *"Not forsaking the assembling of ourselves together... but exhorting one another..."* (Hebrews 10:25, NKJV). Church is not just an event. It is a vital community where believers grow, serve, and support one another.

10. Generational Faith Gap

Younger generations are more likely to question or walk away from faith if it's not deeply rooted, personally experienced, and authentically modeled. A faith that is merely inherited, rather than internalized, often struggles to endure. Scripture calls for intentional generational teaching: *"One generation shall praise Your works to another, and shall declare Your mighty acts"* (Psalms 145:4, NKJV). When faith is lived out authentically, it becomes compelling and transferable across generations.

A Biblical Anchor

Even with these challenges, Scripture gives encouragement: *"As for me and my house, we will serve the Lord"* (Joshua 24:15, NKJV). This declaration is more than a statement. It is a commitment to intentional living. It acknowledges that while the world may shift, a family can remain anchored in God.

The challenge is real, but so is the opportunity. Families that stay intentional about prayer, the Word, communication, and unity can grow stronger even in difficult times. With God at the center, every challenge becomes an invitation to deepen faith, strengthen relationships, and build a lasting spiritual legacy.

Chapter Six

Essential Tools for Investing in the Family

Chapter Six
Essential Tools for Investing in the Family

In order to lay the foundation for a strong, healthy family, there are five building blocks that must be implemented and used routinely, on a daily basis. Without these five building blocks in place, the foundation your family rests upon may not be as strong as you would like it to be. Matthew 7:24 (KJV) states, *"Therefore whosoever heareth these sayings of mine, and doeth them, I will liken him unto a wise man, which built his house upon a rock."* In order for the foundation of your home to firmly stand, it must be built with solid precepts.

1. Understanding Each Other

Understanding is more than simply knowing facts about one another. It is the intentional pursuit of the heart behind the person. It requires listening beyond words, paying attention to tone, body language, and unspoken needs. In a spiritual family, understanding creates safety. It allows each member to feel seen, heard, and valued.

To understand one another, time must be invested. Conversations must go deeper than surface-level exchanges. Ask questions that invite honesty: *What are you feeling? What do you need? What has been weighing on you?* When these questions are asked with sincerity, they open the door for connection rather than assumption.

Misunderstanding often becomes the breeding ground for conflict. When we fail to understand, we begin to interpret through our own lens instead of seeking clarity. But when understanding becomes a daily practice, it diffuses tension before it escalates and strengthens unity before division can take root.

Understanding one another also means recognizing that each person is uniquely designed. Personalities differ. Communication styles vary. Emotional needs are not identical. Taking the time to learn these differences and honoring them builds a culture of respect within the home.

Scripture reminds us in Proverbs 18:13 (KJV), *"He that answereth a matter before he heareth it, it is folly and shame unto him."* This verse emphasizes the importance of listening before responding, seeking understanding before forming conclusions.

2. Intentional Communication

A strong spiritual family does not leave communication to chance. It cultivates it with purpose. Intentional communication means speaking with clarity, listening with patience, and responding with wisdom. It is not just about what is said, but how and when it is said.

Too often, families communicate reactively rather than thoughtfully. Words spoken in frustration can wound deeply and linger far longer than intended. But when communication is intentional, it becomes a tool for building rather than breaking. It creates space for truth without hostility and correction without shame.

Intentional communication also includes active listening. Listening is not simply waiting for your turn to speak. It is fully engaging with the speaker, seeking to understand before responding. When family members feel heard, their defenses lower, and their openness increases.

In a spiritual home, communication should reflect grace. Even difficult conversations can be handled with gentleness and respect. Tone should be guarded, timing should be considered, and motives should be pure. When practiced daily, intentional communication strengthens trust and deepens connection.

The Word of God provides clear instruction in James 1:19 (KJV): *"Wherefore, my beloved brethren, let every man be swift to hear, slow to speak, slow to wrath."* This principle, when applied in the home, transforms conversations and prevents unnecessary conflict.

Additionally, Proverbs 15:1 teaches, *"A soft answer turneth away wrath: but grievous words stir up anger."* Intentional communication guards both tone and timing, ensuring that words bring healing rather than harm.

3. Consistent Prayer and Spiritual Alignment

A spiritual family must be rooted in something greater than individual strength. It must be anchored in God. Consistent prayer invites God into the center of the home, making Him the foundation upon which every decision, conversation, and relationship is built. Prayer is not reserved for crises; it is a daily discipline. It aligns hearts, unifies minds, and creates a shared dependence on God. Whether it is corporate prayer as a family or individual prayer that contributes to the spiritual atmosphere of the home, consistency is key.

Through prayer, burdens are shared, guidance is received, and peace is established. It becomes the place where misunderstandings are softened, where forgiveness is cultivated, and where direction is clarified. A family that prays together develops a spiritual sensitivity that strengthens every other aspect of their relationship.

Spiritual alignment also includes engaging with the Word of God together. Teaching, discussing, and applying biblical principles ensures that the family is not led by emotion or circumstance, but by truth. This alignment creates stability, even in uncertain seasons. In 1 Thessalonians 5:17, we are instructed to *"Pray without ceasing."* This speaks to a lifestyle of prayer, one that is continual, consistent, and sincere.

Furthermore, Joshua 24:15 (KJV) declares, *"But as for me and my house, we will serve the Lord."* This verse establishes the importance of spiritual alignment within the family, making a unified decision to honor and follow God.

4. Forgiveness and Grace

No family is perfect, and offenses - both intentional and unintentional - are inevitable. What distinguishes a strong family is not the absence of conflict, but the presence of forgiveness. Forgiveness is the decision to release resentment and extend grace, even when it is difficult.

Holding onto offense creates distance. It builds walls that hinder communication, disrupt unity, and weaken the foundation of the home. But forgiveness tears those walls down. It restores connection and allows healing to take place.

Grace must accompany forgiveness. While forgiveness releases the offense, grace creates space for growth. It acknowledges that people are in process and that transformation takes time. Extending grace does not excuse behavior, but it does provide room for change without condemnation.

In a spiritual family, forgiveness should be practiced quickly and sincerely. Delayed forgiveness often allows bitterness to take root. But when grace is extended freely, the home becomes a place of restoration rather than rejection.

Colossians 3:13 (KJV) instructs us, *"Forbearing one another, and forgiving one another... even as Christ forgave you, so also do ye."* This sets the standard for forgiveness, not based on feelings, but on Christ's example.

In addition, Ephesians 4:32 (KJV) says, *"And be ye kind one to another, tenderhearted, forgiving one another, even as God for Christ's sake hath forgiven you."* Forgiveness restores connection, while grace sustains it.

5. Shared Responsibility and Servant Leadership

A strong family is not sustained by one person carrying the weight; it thrives when responsibility is shared. Each member plays a role in maintaining the health, order, and spiritual atmosphere of the home. When everyone contributes, the family functions in unity and balance.

Shared responsibility teaches accountability. It reinforces the understanding that every action (or lack of action) impacts the whole. Whether through practical tasks, emotional support, or spiritual leadership, each person has something valuable to offer.

At the heart of shared responsibility is servant leadership. True leadership within the family is not about control or dominance; it is about service. It is demonstrated through humility, sacrifice, and a willingness to meet the needs of others.

Mark 10:45 (KJV) provides the perfect model: *"For even the Son of man came not to be ministered unto, but to minister, and to give his life a ransom for many."* True leadership is expressed through service, humility, and sacrifice.

Additionally, Galatians 6:2 (KJV) encourages, *"Bear ye one another's burdens, and so fulfil the law of Christ."* Shared responsibility ensures that no one carries the weight alone and that the family operates in unity and support.

Servant leadership reflects the model established by Christ, where greatness is defined by the ability to serve. When this principle is embraced within the family, it eliminates competition and fosters cooperation. Each member seeks not only their own well-being, but the well-being of others.

When these five building blocks (understanding, intentional communication, consistent prayer, forgiveness, and shared responsibility) are practiced daily, they create a foundation that is both strong and enduring. Such a family is not easily shaken by trials, because it is built on principles that withstand pressure.

A home constructed in this way becomes more than a dwelling place. It becomes a sanctuary. It becomes a place where love is lived out, where faith is strengthened, and where each member is equipped to grow, thrive, and walk confidently in their God-given purpose.

Chapter Seven

Conversation Building Tools

Chapter Seven
Conversation Building Tools

In many homes, conversations often remain at the surface, centered around schedules, responsibilities, and daily routines. While these exchanges are necessary, they rarely cultivate the depth required to build a truly strong and spiritually grounded family. Meaningful questions, however, have the power to go beyond the surface. They invite honesty, encourage vulnerability, and create opportunities for each family member to be both seen and heard.

This chapter is designed to guide you into those deeper spaces. Before a foundation can be strengthened, there must first be a willingness to examine what currently exists. These questions serve as mirrors, reflecting values, revealing needs, and highlighting areas where growth is both necessary and possible. They create a safe environment for dialogue, one where love is expressed not only through words, but through understanding and intentional engagement.

As you journey through these questions, it is important to approach them with patience and grace. Not every response will come easily, and not every conversation will feel comfortable. However, discomfort often signals that something meaningful is taking place. Growth requires honesty, and honesty requires courage.

The goal is not perfection, but progress. These discussions are meant to draw your family closer, not only to one another, but also to God. As truth is shared and hearts are opened, you will begin to see stronger connections form, deeper compassion develop, and a greater sense of unity emerge.

Here are 50 thoughtful, conversation-stirring questions you can ask a family that are great for gatherings, counseling, or deep discussions. They're designed to spark reflection, connection, and growth. These questions are not merely meant to fill silence or pass time; they are intentional tools crafted to open hearts, uncover hidden thoughts, and strengthen the relational fabric of the family unit.

Faith & Purpose

1. What role does God play in our family decisions?
2. How do we handle challenges spiritually as a family?
3. What legacy of faith do we want to leave behind?
4. When do we feel closest to God as a family?
5. How can we grow spiritually together?

Family Identity & Values

6. What do we stand for as a family?
7. What values are most important to us?
8. How do we want others to describe our family?
9. What traditions define us?
10. Are we living the values we say we believe?

Communication & Relationships

11. Do we truly listen to each other?
12. How do we handle disagreements?
13. Is there anything left unsaid that needs to be shared?
14. Do we create a safe space for honesty?
15. How can we communicate better?

Love & Support

16. How do we show love to one another?
17. Does everyone feel valued and appreciated?
18. When was the last time we encouraged each other?
19. Are we meeting each other's emotional needs?
20. How can we support one another more intentionally?

Growth & Accountability

21. What are we doing to grow individually and together?
22. How do we handle correction or discipline?
23. Are we holding each other accountable in love?

24. What habits need to change in our family?
25. How do we celebrate progress?

Conflict & Forgiveness

26. How do we resolve conflict in a healthy way?
27. Are there any unresolved hurts we need to address?
28. Do we practice forgiveness regularly?
29. What does reconciliation look like for us?
30. Are we quick to apologize and quick to forgive?

Time & Priorities

31. Are we spending enough quality time together?
32. What distractions are pulling us apart?
33. How do we prioritize family time?
34. Are we too busy for what matters most?
35. What changes can we make to be more present?

Stewardship & Responsibility

36. How are we managing our resources as a family?
37. Are we teaching good financial habits?
38. What does generosity look like for us?
39. Are we being faithful stewards of what we have?
40. How can we improve in this area?

Impact & Legacy

41. What impact do we want our family to have on others?
42. Are we serving our community together?
43. What kind of legacy are we building?
44. How do we want to be remembered?
45. Are we making a difference beyond ourselves?

Vision for the Future

46. Where do we see our family in 5–10 years?
47. What goals should we set together?
48. What dreams do we need to pursue as a family?
49. How can we better align our vision?
50. What steps can we take today to build a stronger future?

Chapter Eight

Safeguarding Your Marriage

Chapter Eight
Safeguarding Your Marriage

In a world filled with competing priorities, constant distractions, and shifting values, safeguarding your marriage must become a deliberate pursuit. What you protect, you preserve; and what you consistently invest in, you strengthen. A healthy marriage requires more than love alone. It requires wisdom, discipline, humility, and a shared commitment to honoring God in every aspect of the relationship.

Scripture provides a clear and unchanging foundation for this covenant. It offers guidance not only for navigating challenges, but also for building a relationship marked by unity, respect, and enduring love. As written in Ephesians 5:25 (KJV) , *"Husbands, love your wives, even as Christ also loved the church, and gave himself for it."* This standard calls for a love that is sacrificial, intentional, and unwavering.

Additionally, Ecclesiastes 4:12 (KJV) reminds us, *"A threefold cord is not quickly broken."* When God is at the center of a marriage, He becomes the binding strength that holds it together through every season.

The principles that follow are designed to help you guard what God has entrusted to you. They address communication, trust, intimacy, forgiveness, partnership, and spiritual unity, each one reinforced by the truth of God's Word. As you engage with these practices, approach them not as a checklist, but as a lifestyle. Allow them to shape your actions, refine your perspective, and deepen your connection.

A safeguarded marriage does not mean a perfect marriage, but it does mean a protected one, a union that is continually strengthened, restored when necessary, and grounded in something far greater than emotion alone. As you apply these scriptural principles, you will begin to build a marriage that is resilient, life-giving, and firmly established on a foundation that cannot easily be shaken.

Here are 50 ways to safeguard your marriage, each anchored in Scripture for spiritual strength, wisdom, and daily application: these are not simply principles to admire, but practices to be lived out intentionally, day by day. Marriage does not thrive by accident. It is cultivated through commitment, nurtured through consistency, and sustained through spiritual alignment.

Foundation & Commitment

1. **Put God first together** – Matthew 6:33
2. **Build on a spiritual foundation** – Ecclesiastes 4:12
3. **Commit to covenant, not convenience** – Malachi 2:14

4. **Love unconditionally** – 1 Corinthians 13:4–7
5. **Remain faithful in all things** – Hebrews 13:4

Communication & Respect

6. **Be quick to listen, slow to speak** – James 1:19
7. **Speak with kindness** – Proverbs 15:1
8. **Avoid corrupt communication** – Ephesians 4:29
9. **Speak truth in love** – Ephesians 4:15
10. **Honor and respect each other** – 1 Peter 3:7

Unity & Partnership

11. **Become one flesh in unity** – Genesis 2:24
12. **Agree together in purpose** – Amos 3:3
13. **Bear one another's burdens** – Galatians 6:2
14. **Submit to one another** – Ephesians 5:21
15. **Encourage each other daily** – Hebrews 3:13

Love & Intimacy

16. **Keep romance alive** – Song of Solomon 7:10
17. **Do not deprive one another** – 1 Corinthians 7:5
18. **Rejoice in your spouse** – Proverbs 5:18
19. **Show affection often** – Romans 12:10
20. **Let love be sincere** – Romans 12:9

Prayer & Spiritual Growth

21. **Pray together regularly** – Matthew 18:19
22. **Seek God's wisdom** – James 1:5

23. **Study the Word together** - 2 Timothy 3:16
24. **Worship together** - Joshua 24:15
25. **Trust God in trials** - Proverbs 3:5-6

Conflict Resolution

26. **Forgive quickly** - Colossians 3:13
27. **Do not let anger linger** - Ephesians 4:26
28. **Pursue peace** - Romans 12:18
29. **Avoid strife** - Proverbs 20:3
30. **Overcome evil with good** - Romans 12:21

Protection & Boundaries

31. **Guard your heart** - Proverbs 4:23
32. **Avoid temptation** - 1 Corinthians 10:13
33. **Flee immorality** - 1 Corinthians 6:18
34. **Set healthy boundaries** - 1 Thessalonians 4:3-4
35. **Keep your marriage honorable** - Hebrews 13:4

Growth & Maturity

36. **Grow in patience** - Galatians 5:22
37. **Practice humility** - Philippians 2:3
38. **Serve one another** - Galatians 5:13
39. **Be transformed daily** - Romans 12:2
40. **Walk in the Spirit** - Galatians 5:16

Joy & Gratitude

41. **Give thanks always** - 1 Thessalonians 5:18

42. **Rejoice together** – Philippians 4:4
43. **Celebrate each other's victories** – Romans 12:15
44. **Be content** – Hebrews 13:5
45. **Keep a joyful heart** – Proverbs 17:22

Leadership & Roles

46. **Love sacrificially (husbands)** – Ephesians 5:25
47. **Respect your husband (wives)** – Ephesians 5:33
48. **Lead with wisdom** – Proverbs 24:3
49. **Be a godly example** – 1 Timothy 4:12
50. **Serve the Lord together** – Joshua 25:15

References

Holy Bible (KJV). 2026. www.biblegateway.com.

Holy Bible (NIV). 2026. www.biblegateway.com.

Holy Bible (NKJV). 2026. www.biblegateway.com.

Holy Bible (NLT). 2026. www.biblegateway.com.

Swindoll, Charles. 1977. *You and Your Child*. Nashville: Nelson Pub., pp. 63-64.

About the Author

Bishop Leon Martin has a rich legacy as a father of three children whom he raised with his late wife Dr. Jacqueline Martin. Together, they founded *Love, Peace, and Happiness Christian Fellowship* in 1974, where he has served as the senior pastor for over 50 years.

<u>The Legacy of Bishop Leon Martin</u>

In the late 1960s, after having graduated high school in Houston, Texas, Mr. Leon Martin moved to California with the intent of attending Life Bible College for biblical studies. At the same time, he placed his membership at Ephesians Church of God in Christ, which was under the leadership of the late Bishop E. E. Cleveland, whom Mr. Martin had met when Bishop Cleveland ministered during a visit to Texas.

During the eight years Mr. Martin was a member of Ephesians, he was dedicated to the work of the Lord. He served in several capacities from youth pastor to state president of the Youth Department of the 2nd Jurisdiction under Bishop Cleveland, who was the presiding bishop.

Four years after beginning Life Bible College, Mr. Martin graduated and was subsequently given the opportunity to pastor a church within the Four Square International organization. The offer included a church being provided to him. However, Mr. Martin declined the offer. At that time, after being in ministry, he certainly felt the call of God in his life, but his desire was to operate in the capacity of a traveling evangelist.

Approximately four years later, in 1974, the call of God was very strong. Mr. Martin, who by that time had become ordained as Elder Martin, stepped out on faith and into the pastorship as he, along with his wife Jacqueline Martin founded *Love, Peace, and Happiness Family Christian Fellowship*. The church was organized in their home, which was in Compton, California. There, on Tuesday nights, Bible study was held. At the same time, Pastor Martin reached out to Superintendent Harold Conedy of Palm Lane Church of God in Christ, seeking a place to have worship services with his newly-attained members.

Superintendent Conedy was more than willing to lend a helping hand. For the next year or so, *Love, Peace, and Happiness Family Christian Fellowship* was held on Saturdays within the building of Palm Lane Church. Approximately one or two years later, Pastor Martin ushered his members into their own church building located at 7225 Walnut Drive in Los Angeles, California. From 1974 to present day 2024, *Love, Peace, and Happiness Family Christian Fellowship* grew to four locations. Bishop Leon Martin has been in ministry for 50 years and is still standing faithful. Let's reflect upon his ministry decade by decade.

First Decade (1974-1983)

Ministry does not come without challenges, and pastoring is certainly without exception. Once Pastor Martin set his heart to start a church, one of the first challenges he faced was securing a building. God blessed him and the flock with a location at 7225 Walnut Drive in Los Angeles, California. With a new home for *Love, Peace, and Happiness Family Christian Fellowship*, Pastor Martin then found himself tasked with bringing in the harvest. As he was determined to do a work for the Lord, he set out to increase the church's membership, so he could pour the Word of God into the members.

Unfortunately, growth was not occurring at the rate Pastor Martin desired. The location he had chosen was aptly named "A Pastor's Graveyard," because pastor after pastor had attempted to build a church in that location only to find that a force was working against them. Pastor Martin, however, was determined to overcome the challenge.

Using his God-given drive and tenacity, Pastor Martin began to attend The Pastor School designed for pastors who wanted a better understanding of how to win the harvest. At the evangelistic trainings, held in Hammond, Indiana, Pastor Martin gained the necessary tools with which to win the lost, the uncommitted, the unchurched, and the untaught. With the newly attained information, the focus of the ministry became soul winning. To assist in the endeavor, Pastor Martin purchased five buses and took to the streets, gathering those who were hungry for a change in their lives. Each week, the buses brought many visitors to the church, and many of them joined, getting their needs for the love of God and His Word fulfilled. The Sunday school department grew to over 800 members.

Unfortunately, the challenges Pastor Martin experienced did not end with a desire to increase membership. No, that was simply the tip of the iceberg. As the membership slowly increased, the financial need also increased. Because there were no investors or underwriters for the ministry, the financial responsibility fell entirely to Pastor Martin. The membership contributed what they could by way of tithes and offerings, but most of the members were young and therefore did not have an abundance of finances. Week after week and month after month, the financial strain weighed on Pastor Martin, and just when the point came to make a decision, he pondered whether or not it would be best for him and his young family to let the ministry go and return to working full time. To assist in his decision, the Holy Spirit intervened, making it clear that He was the one who called Pastor Martin into ministry and that He had assigned a work to his hands. Receiving the confirmation from the Lord, Pastor Martin held steadfast in obedience to God and refrained from throwing his hands up and walking away.

Decade Two (1984-1993)

Moving to Pastor Martin's second decade of pastoring, from 1984-1993, he was yet preaching the gospel in his first location on Walnut Drive. But his presence there would not remain for much longer. Eventually, as the ministry continued to add new members, the congregation outgrew that location, and Pastor Martin set his sights on a location that could house the present members and those that would come in the future. Feeling the presence of the Holy Spirit guiding him, Pastor Martin launched a mega evangelistic outreach by hosting a citywide tent crusade in the city of Los Angeles. Although experience in tent meetings and revivals was not on his side, the Holy Spirit was. Many souls and many new members attended the tent meeting and many joined the church. And although Pastor Martin could not be more filled with joy with the outcome of the crusade, not everything was going well.

Unfortunately, the ministry took a backset when the church's bus driver was involved in a traffic collision while driving the bus. Incidentally, the insurance company cancelled the church's insurance policy. Pastor Martin had no choice but to retire the buses from picking up the harvest. That effect remained in place for over ten years. However, the backset would not debilitate Pastor Martin from forging forward. To accommodate the growing ministry, Pastor Martin left Walnut Drive and moved the members to 8606 Menlo (in Los Angeles), where they would remain for two years. During that same time frame, he purchased nine lots and had architectural plans drawn up to build a new facility. The facility was designed to consist of multiple buildings to include a main church, an educational facility, and a large parking lot.

Sadly, due to a lack of funding, the building project was slow to get off the ground. Eventually, Pastor Martin went into prayer to obtain direction from the Lord. Afterall, the Word says, *"If any of you lack wisdom, let him ask of God, that giveth to all men liberally, and upbraideth not; and it shall be given him"* (James 1:5). After much prayer, Pastor Martin released the project.

Not much later, the owner of a stationary store was retiring from his business and asked Pastor Martin if he would like to purchase the building to hold church services. Pastor Martin readily consented, and the church moved once again. That time, the move was to Manchester Avenue in Los Angeles. At that time during Pastor Martin's ministry, he was on fire for the Lord and still possessed a zeal for saving souls. The Lord spoke to his heart and instructed him to open a church location in the city of Rialto (in the Inland Empire of Southern California). Also, the membership in Los Angeles was steadily growing. The one church service in Los Angeles expanded to two services to accommodate all the church members.

Therefore, there were a total of three services that Pastor Martin preached each Sunday. He would begin his day in Los Angeles, drive to Rialto, and then close the day out in Los Angeles.

Although there were certainly challenges Pastor Martin faced during his second decade of pastoring, the good abundantly outweighed the bad! His heart was in the right place, and his head was consistently uplifted toward the hills because he knew his help and his strength came from the Lord (Psalm 121:1-2).

Decade Three (1994-2003)

Progressing along our journey through Pastor Martin's years of pastoring, we travel in time to the third decade (1994-2003) of his ministerial work. With the guidance of the Holy Spirit, Pastor Martin, who was ordained as a bishop during this decade, answered the call of God to launch a church in the Inland Empire of Southern California (as mentioned in the last section). That location of *Love, Peace, and Happiness Family Christian Fellowship* began in the city of San Bernardino at a hotel with only a few members. After a few months, the "church" was moved to a small commercial building. However, the membership quickly outgrew the space. As a result, Bishop Martin obtained the additional units of the commercial building (four in total), thereby expanding the square footage of the church, allowing room for continual growth of the flock.

As time progressed, the favor of the Lord shone on both the Los Angeles location and the Rialto location. Eventually, with further growth in Rialto, an additional suite, in the same commercial complex, was obtained because the youth department had grown in size, matching the number of adult members. Under the leadership of the youth pastor, Carlos Martin, their activities caused them to need their own space. Meanwhile, the "west" location, as it was affectionally called, shifted from Los Angeles to Downey, making Downey the new headquarters of the church. With this advancement in the ministry, shifting members from their comfort in Los Angeles to the city of Downey, the church took an unfortunate hit, losing approximately 25% of its membership.

However, Bishop Martin was not deterred; rather, he was determined to regrow the membership and to exceed the previous count. So, he returned to one of his passions- outreach through the bus ministry- to reach his desired goal. To ensure the success of the outreach ministry, Bishop Martin purchased four buses, and the bus ministry, which had lay dormant for nearly fifteen years, was relaunched. At that time, the Extended Hands Ministry was birthed. This was a component of the Outreach Ministry that picked up guests from Downtown Los Angeles to minister to their spiritual and physical needs, by providing access to the Word of God and a hot meal for the day. Soon, the Downey location saw exponential growth, and on some Sundays, all the pews would be filled, causing chairs to be added down the aisles to accommodate all members and guests. At that point, both locations, Rialto and Downey were thriving.

Decade Four (2004-2013)

As we move forward to the next decade, surveying 2004-2013, Bishop Martin continued to stay in the press toward the mark of the high calling of God in Christ Jesus. He was consistently proving himself to be steadfast and unmovable, as he abounded in the work of the Lord. Although challenges continued to make their way into his territory, he did not succumb to them. He was determined to please God rather than man or himself because it was God who called him into ministry, not man. So, despite personal challenges and human inadequacy, Bishop Martin remained faithful to God, nurturing and teaching the flock the Word of God and how to apply it to their lives. All in all, Bishop Martin walked in total dedication to his earthly, God-given assignment.

One of the developments, shifts and changes in the ministry included Bishop Martin installing his eldest son Pastor Carlos Martin, along his wife Lady Fatima Martin, as the senior pastor of the Rialto location in 2005. For the next seven years, the two locations (Downey and Rialto) thrived. Then, around 2010, Bishop Martin opened a third location for the church in the city of Los Angeles on 54th Street. After one year, the church shifted from that location to 4951 S. Figueroa Avenue, also in Los Angeles, where it remains today. The first service was held on Easter Sunday. That move came as an extreme blessing when the members had the opportunity to take possession of a brand-new church that had been fully designed and decorated, without ever having a church service held there.

Decade Five (2014-2024)

In 2014, Bishop heard the voice of the Lord again. That time, he was instructed to return to the city of Compton and open a fourth location. In obedience, the church was launched in July of that year. Then, a shift came that would rattle the ministry like no other change in the ministry before. The beloved Downey location, that had been a major part of the ministry for approximately twenty years or more, closed its doors, hosting the last service on Mother's Day of 2018. With the close came another shift in the ministry, spreading the Downey members to either the Los Angeles location or the Compton location. To God be the glory because the sheep were not without a church home.

That same year, in 2018, First Lady Dr. Jacqueline Martin fell ill. The physical challenges she experienced led to adjustments being made in the ministry. The companionship and assistance in ministry Bishop Martin had grown accustomed to from his wife over the previous decades greatly shifted. In 2020, the worldwide COVID-19 pandemic caused a great shift in churches throughout our land, and was the catalyst for the doors of the Compton location being closed. The Rialto location went online, using social media platforms as a way to continue spreading the gospels to members, friends, and guests each week. However, the doors of the Los Angeles location remained open, and the church began live streaming the services for members who elected to worship in the comfort and safety of their homes. All of the members of the *Love, Peace, and Happiness Family Christian Fellowship* remained connected with the fellowship, and many engaged in daily prayer via the morning family prayer line, continuing to be enhanced spiritually and encouraged throughout the trying and uncertain times the world at large faced.

Throughout the pandemic and the subsequent years, the church experienced much death, including the Minister of Music, Kelvin Jones and one of the elders, Derek Edwards. Then, in March 2022, the *Love, Peace, and Happiness Family Christian Fellowship* suffered the loss of First Lady Dr. Jacqueline Martin as she transitioned from this earthly realm to her heavenly abode. Her passing caused a hard hit on the ministry and upon her loving husband, children, and grandchildren.

Then, one of the faithful Family Matters pastors, Pastor Isaac Thompson succumbed to his health challenges only two weeks later. The death angel continued to hover, causing another great loss when the chairman of the deacon board, Deacon Willie Smith was called to glory in 2023. During that season from 2020 to 2023, others passed as well. Each and every one is missed, and their contribution to the ministry will be remembered.

During the post-pandemic period, *Love, Peace, and Happiness Family Christian Fellowship* began the road of recovery. The Compton location resumed services in early 2022. The ministry took on the spirit of evangelism with enhanced outreach programs, including door-to-door witnessing. The ministry experienced a redevelopment of the convalescent ministry. The direct mail program was revamped, and the media ministry was launched, focusing on social media efforts being taken to a higher level of engagement. The members of the congregation began to return to all three locations with the spirit of enthusiasm and excitement from once again being in fellowship with other believers. Throughout the ministry, everyone understood God is not done with *Love, Peace, and Happiness Family Christian Fellowship*. The best is yet to come, and the future of the ministry is looking brighter.

As we look to the future, Bishop Martin remains on the radio every Sunday morning on KJLH, continuing to use the platform as part of the evangelistic thrust of the ministry. He began his 30-minute segments approximately seven years ago; however, he was not new to radio at that time. He actually began his radio broadcast in 1976 with a five-day a week broadcast on KTYM.

Throughout his nearly 50-year broadcast, Bishop Martin has touched lives numbering in the tens of thousands, adding more sheep into the sheepfold daily. As the *Love, Peace, and Happiness Family Christian Fellowship* continues to press toward the mark, Bishop Martin endeavors to develop more community-involvement programs, including redesigning the Extended Hands Ministry, which is a program caring to the needs of the unhoused; redeveloping the bus ministry to bring members of the community to worship services; continuing the bill pay ministry; and is looking to develop other programs to meet the needs of the community, including job and housing assistance.

Over the past 50 years of ministry, being a dreamer and self motivator, Bishop Martin has accomplished everything and more his heart desired as it relates to ministry. However, he never would have dreamed he would establish four locations after laying the foundation for the first one. With his willing spirit, he will go wherever God sends him.

At the beginning of his pastoral ministry, Bishop Martin was blessed to have several faithful supporters, including Burinedean Flanagan and family; Geraldine Nichols-Blackwell; Pastor Ronald Harris; Jerry Lee and family; Pastor Wayne Pittman and family; Shirley Dubois; Thomas and Dorothy Stone; Arthur and Archie Nichols and family.

Furthermore, there were other ministers of the gospel who inspired Bishop Martin throughout his ministry, including Jack Hyles, of the First Baptist Church in Hammond, Indiana, who convened a school for pastors from all over the nation, with 25,000 people in attendance and over 100 buses; Pastor Tommy Burnett of Phoenix, Arizona, who was also inspired by Jack Hyles; Bishop Charles Blake of West Angeles Church of God in Christ; Pastor Robert Schuler of Crystal Cathedral in Orange County, California; the late Apostle Fred Price of Crenshaw Christian Center in Los Angeles, California; Dr. I.V. Hilliard of New Light Christian Center in Houston, Texas; and Pastor Rick Warren of Saddleback Church in Lake Forest, California.

Looking back over the past fifty years, Bishop Martin is forever grateful, thankful, and humbled that God chose him to lead in His vineyard. He counts his experiences as a blessing because he was able to see the move of God over and over again, even after starting with zero, by taking a giant leap of faith. According to Bishop Martin, every phase of the ministry has been a miracle performed by the hand of God, from seeing numerical growth of lives saved and changed, marriages restored, people healed, and financial blessings falling upon the membership.

As stated earlier, ministry has not come without challenges. For Bishop Martin, the greatest challenge he endured was having a lack of finances. There were and still are a great many ideas he has in his mind and heart to carry out for the ministry, but with financial constraints, he has been unable to do so. But, his faith is strong, and he is yet believing his desires will come to fruition. So, onward he marches!

www.ingramcontent.com/pod-product-compliance
Lightning Source LLC
LaVergne TN
LVHW052338100826
845147LV00020B/1105

* 9 7 9 8 9 9 2 5 7 8 4 4 7 *